The
Elijah
Factor

ISBN 978-1-954095-85-4

The Elijah Factor: A Call To Boldness

Copyright ©2021 John Parish

Unless otherwise noted, all Scriptures are taken from the King James Version (KJV).

For permission requests, write to the publisher at the address below.

Yorkshire Publishing
4613 E. 91st St,
Tulsa, OK 74137
www.YorkshirePublishing.com
918.394.2665

Printed in the USA

The Elijah Factor

(A CALL TO BOLDNESS)

JOHN PARISH

TULSA

CONTENTS

ACKNOWLEDGMENT

With a heart full of gratitude, I wish to acknowledge the faithful support of two of God's most choice servants, Don and Janet Mellott, who have sacrificed and labored to expand the Kingdom of God in so many ways for so many years.

Their vision and sensitivity to leadership of the Holy Spirit is directly responsible for the publication of this book.

"For God is not unrighteous to forget your work and labour of love, which ye have shewed toward his name, in that ye have ministered to the saints, and do minister." (Hebrews 6:10)

May the Lord reward them greatly for every heart who is touched with the transforming information contained in this manuscript.

Pastor John Parish
Senior Pastor
Lighthouse Christian Center

INTRODUCTION

An article appeared in the December 15, 1990, edition of the *Jerusalem Post* reporting on the strange extraterrestrial phenomena taking place around Mt. Carmel, the mountain where Elijah called fire down from Heaven.

UFO sightings are common in Israel, but the reports about the strange activities on Mt. Carmel were not ordinary sightings of strange objects in the night sky. Two witnesses at different times described something that appeared as a "pillar of fire" hovering close to the ground. The ground was examined the next day and it was discovered the vegetation in the area was scorched by some type of radiation.

Just days from the first sighting on the eve of Rosh Hashanah in 1987, another sighting occurred. The witness said that the object appeared as a ring of fire hovering close enough to the ground for him to hear it. He described the sound as a "rushing wind."

On another occasion, ten Israeli soldiers reported seeing something they described as a "chariot of fire" traveling across the sky.

Hundreds of similar reports prompted the Haifa Police Department to enlist the help of an Israeli expert on UFOs, Ha▓▓▓▓▓▓▓▓▓▓▓▓investigate. Her conclusions were astounding. After interviewing multiple witnesses and examining the area where these sightings occurred, she noted that these strange events were all happening on Jewish holidays. The "pillar of fire" and objects spewing white sparks were seen at Rosh Hashanah, Pesach, and Succoth. All of these UFO sightings happened near Elijah's cave on Mount Carmel.

Her official report said that these phenomena appear to be "signals of some kind." She concluded that extraterrestrial vehicles in flaming fire appearing on Mount Carmel are linked to Malachi's ancient prophecy of Elijah's return.

She surmised that since Elijah left the earth in a chariot of fire, he will return in a similar way, and all the sightings seen on Mount Carmel were indicating the time for Malachi's prophecy was near.

Since that series of extraterrestrial occurrences over three decades ago, prophetic events in Israel have accelerated until the world is now positioned for the final seven years of this age.

It is not yet time for Elijah to complete the ministry which was interrupted in centuries past, but prophetic signs undeniably verify that the Endtimes are now upon us, and dramatic manifestations of God's power are ordained to happen in the "spirit and power of Elijah."

An important dimension of the Holy Spirit's operations in these perilous times can be understood from something which the Apostle Paul wrote to the Corinthians. The Apostle identified himself as "one born out of due time" (I Cor. 15:8). He viewed his conversion and ministry as preliminary to the time when "all Israel shall be saved" (Rom. 11:26).

Actually, his ministry was a prototype of the 144,000 Jewish witnesses who will impact the world during the first part of the coming seven years of Tribulation (Rev. 7). The precedent was set at the very beginning of this dispensation that God's people in present times will experience foretastes of future anointings and coming glory. The Apostle Paul's ministry was a precursor of the ministries which will happen in the future Tribulation. Redeemed believers should expect earth-shaking manifestations of God's power in these perilous times. Joel's ancient prophecy is that an outpouring of divine glory will occur in "the last days" that makes "sons and daughters" prophesy (Joel 2:28).

The prophesied Tribulation period will begin with a specific event. The prophet Daniel revealed a coming world ruler will emerge from Europe (the area that once comprised the Roman Empire) to negotiate a seven-year peace pact in the Mideast, convincing Israelis that hostilities against them will end and secure "peace and safety" for their war-torn country (Dan. 9:27). But it will be a false peace intended to lull Israel into a false security as this world ruler plans genocide against the Jewish state.

This event is set to happen in the not-too-distant future. However, the spirit of antichrist is already controlling the globalist policies of nations, setting the stage for the emergence of the diabolic leader called "the man of sin" (II Thess. 2:3).

The politically correct and "woke" spirit of antichrist has overrun the institutions to the point where the devilish New World Order is a foregone conclusion. Not only is there a pre-Tribulation spirit of antichrist loose in the land, but pre-tribulation perversions are driving the culture.

The Lord informed the Apostle Paul that the majority of Earth's teeming billions will have a "seared conscience" in the Endtimes and will refuse every overture of the Holy Spirit to bring them to repentance (I Tim. 4:1-2). The Scripture explicitly reveals four major abominations which will dominate the earth during those coming dark days: "Neither repented they of their murders, nor of their sorceries, nor of their fornication, nor of their thefts" (Rev. 9:21).

When the language of the Scripture is put in modern vernacular, it is clear that the Lord was speaking about drugs (sorcery), abortion (murder), sexual perversions (fornication), and across-the-board corruption (thefts).

These societal factors constitute the "mystery of law-lessness" which is already at work attacking all opposition to the "woke culture" of antichrist. The Tribulation has not yet begun, but the wicked conditions and perversions predicted for those fateful seven years is already widespread.

The Spirit of God working through the Blood-washed Church of Jesus Christ will hinder the ultimate takeover of this demonic lawlessness until God divinely removes believers from this judgment-bound world. The promise recorded in Second Thessalonians 2:7 states that the Spirit-empowered Church will be "taken out of the way."

Jesus will descend as far as the lower atmosphere to command the committed "new creatures in Christ" to come up higher. The Word of the Lord refers to this event as "the catching away" in First Thessalonians 4:16. Other Scriptures speak of this event as "our gathering together unto Him" and "the blessed hope," but it is most commonly referred to as "the Rapture."

We are already witnessing a pre-Tribulation hostile takeover of the culture by the spirit of antichrist. Pre-Tribulation lawlessness is emerging at an alarming rate. All the pre-Tribulation abominations listed in the prophetic books of Daniel and Revelation are escalating. Bible believers are watching the beginnings of the hour that Jesus described as an unparalleled time of wickedness and upheaval (Matt. 24:21).

The Lord gave clear instruction that "when these things begin to come to pass, then look up, and lift up your heads; for your redemption draweth nigh" (Luke 21:28). With all of the pre-Tribulation activity now occurring, the redeemed Church is to expect a pre-Tribulation rapture to transport us from earth to Glory in "the twinkling of an eye."

But there is another pre-Tribulation phenomenon at work. The final prophecy of the Old Testament is that the prophet Elijah will appear before "the great and dreadful day of the Lord" (Mal. 4:5). The timing for Elijah's confrontational and controversial ministry is during the first half of Tribulation. He is one of the witnesses described in Revelation 11:3, who will smite the earth with multiple plagues as he resists the global ambitions of antichrist and exposes the evil of an apostate global religion.

Elijah will oppose the agenda of the world ruler in the same fashion as he contested with King Ahab and the prophets of Baal. Although this famed Old Testament prophet of divine power has not yet arrived, and believers will never see him on the earth, a pre-Tribulation anointing of the Holy Spirit, in the way that Elijah was anointed, is ordained to empower the Church for the challenges of these last days.

Just as John the Baptist ministered in "the spirit and power of Elijah," forerunners of the Rapture will be sent to prepare people for the coming of the Lord. Pre-Tribulation abominations will be hindered by pre-Tribulation demonstrations of the Holy Ghost before "the great and dreadful day of the Lord comes."

The results of the final outpouring will be the mobilization and deployment of a victorious spiritual army in "the spirit and power of Elijah." The time for this miraculous intervention of God's divine Glory has come. Unprecedented upheaval is already moving the world at a rapid rate to the horrors of Tribulation, but divine manifestations of the Holy Ghost will keep the forces of darkness from a total takeover until believers are miraculously removed.

Our archenemy is presently resurrecting old heresies and abominations that were responsible for the destruction of past civilizations. All of the present demonic ideologies have their roots in ancient Baal worship. This devilish belief system was a constant plague to Israel throughout its long history. The Lord raised up the prophet Elijah to confront those who propagated it and to call a deceived nation back to a right relationship with the true God. A special measure of Holy Ghost anointing is desperately needed now to endow God's covenant people with the boldness and power to defeat the modern prophets of Baal.

The purpose of this book is to give enlightenment concerning God's response to the spiritual and moral chaos of the times, and inform believers as to the nature of the last outpouring of the Holy Spirit "before the great and dreadful day of the Lord."

CHAPTER ONE

Before the Coming of the Great and Dreadful Day of the Lord

What's next?

What do we do now?

How much worse will it get?

How much longer will this last?

Is there any hope that things will change?

Will we ever get back to normal?

These are the perplexing and agonizing questions which prey on the minds of frustrated believers as we witness the rapid collapse of our culture and the speedy disintegration of our nation's spiritual infrastructure.

It should be clear to every Christian with even a rudimentary understanding of Bible prophecy that the world is now on the fast track to Tribulation times.

The final seven years of this age will be characterized by unprecedented hatred, violence, perversion, and lawlessness which lead to the totalitarian reign of a world dictator in a New World Order.

The Scripture calls this coming global leader "the beast, the man of sin, and the antichrist." These names reveal the true ~~█████████~~ dividual who will unleash the greatest atrocities the world has ever known.

He will be totally opposite from the image portrayed by the media and government.

He will be hailed as the great peacemaker in persuading warring nations of the Mideast to make a pact with Israel, but the prophet Daniel warns that he "by peace shall destroy many" (Dan. 8:25).

He will be exalted as the master diplomat, the new Caesar, and the only man capable of solving the world's intractable economic and social problems. But all of his elaborate programs are really just a smoke screen to hide his real agenda of genocide and his goal of obliterating the very memory of God from the face of the earth.

For the last three and a half years of Tribulation, he will be worshipped as the world's new god and not tolerate the existance of any other faith.

Yet, before that day arrives when this diabolic figure ascends to world prominence, all the factors that characterize the final seven years of this age will emerge to dominate society and the culture. An antichrist spirit will control government, direct educational institutions, influence multinational corporations, corrupt religious denominations, guide the media, and even reach into the Church, producing a nauseating mindset that God has promised to vomit out (Rev. 3:16).

The spirit of antichrist is propagating a new global religion that is presently spreading its evil tentacles into every segment of society. It is responsible for stealing a presidential election, exploiting a spurious pandemic to stampede an unsuspecting public into fear-stricken submission, and legitimizing a cancel culture that is insane with hatred of everything godly and Biblical.

It is destroying our constitutional liberties, censoring freedom of speech, strangling Bible believers with detestable restrictions, distorting the Gospel, and poisoning the minds of the masses with a toxic philosophy that subverts all decency and morality.

It hides under such innocuous names as "social justice" and "racial equity," but there is nothing just or righteous about it.

This new religion has turned America into a pressure cooker of subversion where stress has reached unbearable levels. There is no remedy to be found in our corrupted institutions which are hopelessly broken.

Some misguided individuals are desperately holding onto the vain hope that moral sanity can still be restored through our political and judicial system. They just don't know, or are unwilling to admit, how deep the corruption now runs through the institutions.

The cancer brought on by America's new religion has metastasized in the Body Politic, and there is none who call for the balm of Gilead (Jer. 8:22).

Isaiah's prophetic words totally capture the conditions which tyrannize our time. . . . "None calleth for justice, nor any pleadeth for truth: they trust in vanity, and speak lies; they conceive mischief, and bring forth iniquity...their works are works of iniquity, and the act of violence is in their hand. Their feet run to evil, and they make haste to shed innocent blood: their thoughts are thoughts of iniquity; wasting and destruction are in their paths. The way of peace they know not; and there is no judgment in their goings: they have made them crooked paths: whosoever goeth therein shall not know peace. Therefore is judgment far from us, neither doth justice overtake us: we wait for light, but behold obscurity; for brightness, but we walk in darkness...Yea, truth faileth; and he that departeth from evil maketh himself a prey: and the Lord saw it, and it displeased him that there was no judgement" (Isa. 59:4, 6-9, 15).

Social engineers have identified America's new state religion as "wokeness." It is a global religion intent on destroying America's sovereignty, its Constitution, its freedom, its exceptionalism, and—worst of all—its faith in the God of the Bible.

Born-again, Bible-believing Christians are the primary obstacle, hindering this new religion from a complete takeover of the nation. It is no exaggeration or conspiracy theory to state that this woke antichrist religion has targeted believers for ethnic cleansing and genocide. The ethnic cleansing is happening now. The genocide is planned for later.

White House executive orders are intended to disarm the public and leave the country defenseless to their socialist agenda. The military is being purged of all Christian influences. West Point cadets and even rank-and-file troops are currently indoctrinated in "woke" globalism. Our children are subjected to new curricula that teach them to hate the country and its Biblical foundation. Critical Race Theory is rewriting history, portraying America as a hopelessly racist country. The educational establishment has employed brainwashing techniques to goad the next generation into accepting the notion that our country must be obliterated for the greater good of the world community.

Every time politicians talk about "systemic racism" they are accusing the American system of being built on racial hatred, and advocating Marxism as a needed replacement of our constitutional republic. Demonically-inspired professors and politicians are vociferously attempting to deceive the public with the notion that atheistic socialism is a better alternative to a social order based on Judeo-Christian values.

The perilous times foretold by the Apostle Paul are here: "...evil men and seducers shall wax worse and worse, deceiving, and being deceived" (II Tim. 3:13).

It is as Daniel foretold, "the transgressors are come to the full" (Dan. 8:23), setting the stage for the sinister schemes of the world ruler.

The promise that Jesus will call His redeemed to meet Him in the air before "the man of sin" emerges with his diabolic plans of global control is iron clad. No one can believe otherwise who rightly divides the Word of Truth (I Thess. 4:16, II Thess. 2:7). The Lord is coming soon, but what do we do in the meantime?

The Lord addressed two types of churches which for a short period will co-exist before the seven-year Tribulation begins. He spoke of a Philadelphian church with an "open door" for revival and world evangelism. But sadly, that church will diminish until it has "little strength" and eventually be replaced by an increasingly lukewarm ecclesiastical sham.

The final church addressed in Revelation is called Laodicea. The name means "ruled by the people." It is characterized by compromise and obsessed with material gain. This church is "Christian" in name only and has slammed its door on the Lord Jesus. It teaches "things which they ought not, for filthy lucre's sake" (Titus 1:11) and is filled with "false teachers…who privily shall bring in damnable heresies, even denying the Lord that bought them…" (II Peter 2:1).

The words "filthy lucre" is an old English expression for "money gained by dishonest methods." The word "privily" is not used much in modern times. It means secretly and stealthily. The Spirit of God used both the Apostle Paul and the Apostle Peter to inform believers of religious con men motivated by greed that would deceive multitudes with a redefined Gospel which denies the deity and Lordship of Jesus.

In spite of the popular trends toward apostasy, the remnant of the Philadelphian church will "earnestly contend for the faith which was once delivered unto the saints" (Jude 1:3) and be dogmatic in rejecting all compromising trends. Jesus promised to keep that church from the hour of temptation, or Tribulation (Rev. 3:10). The picture given in Revelation chapter three is of a remnant group of believers who stand up to the pressure of the times and overcome all attempts to pervert the Gospel in the midst of wholesale defections from the Faith. According to the Scripture, those tenacious, uncompromising believers will be "kept by the power of God through faith unto salvation ready to be revealed in the last time" (I Peter 1:5). They will ultimately be caught up to meet the Lord in the air before the unrestrained wrath of God falls on a condemned world (I Thess. 4:16, I Thess. 5:9).

The false church will be spued out into horrendous calamities. The true Church will not experience even one day of the events described from Revelation 6 to Revelation 19. These chapters detail the period of time known as Tribulation. Students of Bible prophecy have ignored the fact that conditions of Tribulation times don't start on "day one" of the prophesied seven years. The evil influences, wickedness, disgusting abominations, twisted ideas, warped practices, and demented personal and political behavior characteristic of the Tribulation will control the culture even before the Lord Jesus appears in the clouds to call the redeemed to come up higher.

The Lord informed believers that the Endtimes will witness a resurgence of the corruption and rebellion which existed in Noah's day. The Master stated that social conditions will degenerate to the level of abominations which ruled the cultures of Sodom and Gomorrah in Lot's time. Such lawlessness sets the stage for the appearance of antichrist. Deplorable, unrestrained evil actually constitutes a sign to the remnant that our "redemption is drawing near."

These factors, along with wars, rumors of wars, upheaval of nature, fearful sights in the heavens, bizarre weather, and mysterious pandemics comprise "the beginning of sorrows" in God's prophetic timeline. All of the prophetic signs which the Lord told us to watch for are now in play. The present global culture is exactly as the Word of God foretold it would be, indicating that the Coming of the Lord is near, "even at the door."

The dominant factor of the Endtimes is deception.

Multitudes will be deceived out of their liberty, out of their rights, out of their freedom, and even out of their salvation with sinister philosophies that seem so intellectual and will be promoted as "socially just." Wokeness has suddenly burst on the scene to replace Biblical truth and blind the minds of multitudes. The result of the pervasive acceptance of this demonic philosophy will turn this nation into a lawless "hell on earth."

Wokeness is a major contributing factor to the sorrow, frustration, and bondage of these times. The term "woke" was first coined in the 1940s, but its definition keeps expanding until today it is equivalent to violent Marxist revolution. The riots, destruction, and violent deaths in the so-called "peaceful" protests around the country are examples of "woke" events.

When this new religion is examined in the light of the Scripture, it is evident that this modern religion isn't new at all. Wokeness is actually re-packaged Baal worship. Baalism was the sinister, politically-correct religion of Ahab and Jezebel, the worst of ancient Israel's monarchs.

This diabolical duo reshaped Israel with their devilish religion, just as the pundits and politicians are "fundamentally" changing America today.

Ahab and Jezebel demanded that Baal worship replace the faith of the One True God in ancient Israel. In today's America, college professors, media commentators, and neo-communists in government are demanding that wokeness replace Bible Christianity.

God raised up the prophet Elijah to expose the evil of this demonic philosophy. Elijah appeared unexpectedly, out of nowhere, to announce the judgments of God upon Israel because they turned from Him to serve Baal.

Elijah stood alone to challenge the false prophets of Baal. He repaired the broken altar of God and called fire down on a water-baptized sacrifice. He then brought an abrupt end to the false religion of Baal by slaying its prophets with the sword. Hearing a sound of an abundance of rain, he interceded in prayer until a cloud formed out of the sea and brought rain to a drought-stricken land. He then received supernatural strength to out-run Ahab's chariot, and was ultimately caught up to Heaven.

Elijah was unique among the prophets because of the many miracles that punctuated his message. Divine intervention and displays of righteous judgments followed the word which the Lord commissioned him to speak.

The final prophecy in the Old Testament is about Elijah in the Endtimes. The Lord will send Elijah back to earth again. His miraculous ministry will turn the hearts of children and parents back to the maligned, rejected, and blasphemed faith of their forefathers.

The Word of the Lord is clear that Elijah will appear

"before the coming of the great and dreadful day of the Lord" (Mal. 4:5).

Malachi's prophecy identifies Elijah as one of the two witnesses which John writes about in the Revelation (Rev. 11:3). He will stand with the other witness to defy the antichrist and his evil works. He will contest against antichrist as he did against Ahab and Jezebel centuries ago.

The spirit of antichrist is already ruling institutions, corporations, and even governments. The Apostle John emphasized that the Endtimes would witness "many antichrists; whereby we know that it is the last time" (I John 2:18).

There is a plethora of Ahabs and Jezebels in today's culture. Some can be found in the halls of Congress, others are sitting behind teachers' desks in classrooms, some are presiding over corporate boardrooms, and others appear daily on network newscasts. Their blasphemous posts can be read on social platforms, while high-tech Baal worshipers invent new devices to deceive and control the masses. The spiritual descendants of Ahab and Jezebel occupy influential positions across the entire spectrum of today's society.

The 21st century Ahabs and Jezebels are very vocal and easily identifiable, but where are the Elijahs of God? Where are those witnesses who are supernaturally empowered to resist, expose, and defeat the modern prophets of Baal? Where are the sons and daughters of the Most High with faith and authority to call fire down from Heaven?

Malachi's prophecy is about more than the person of Elijah. It is also about the "spirit of Elijah." His attitude and determination to confront the forces of darkness are vital components of the Spirit's fresh anointing. The raw power of the Holy Ghost seen on Elijah's ministry is needed again to empower God's appointed Endtime witnesses at this critical time.

We can deduce from the volume of prophetic Scriptures that "Last Day witnesses" will be given special anointings in a similar manner as the Holy Ghost anointed this Old Testament prophet whose ministry spans the ages. The singular purpose of this special anointing is to equip believers to fight and conquer the evil of modern Baalism. At the very beginning of the church age, God wrought special miracles by the hands of Paul (Acts 19:11). Such special anointings and miraculous manifestations will happen again in "the spirit and power of Elijah."

It is tragic that believers have forgotten the emphasis which Jesus placed on receiving power from on high. His last urgent command before ascending to the Father's right hand was for the disciples to tarry until endued with Heaven's supernatural and miraculous abilities. Jesus impressed on the disciples that mighty changes were coming when the Holy Ghost arrived. They would be transformed into His Church and become "witnesses" equipped with divine glory to reach the uttermost parts of the earth (Acts 1:8).

As prophetic events accelerate, believers should recognize that present conditions require more than a tepid, lukewarm relationship with Jesus. The status quo is no longer effective in reaching a lost world. The unique peril of these last days has produced a calloused generation which has hardened itself to the Gospel and seems impervious to the touch of the Holy Spirit. If the Church is to accomplish its mission in these dark times, then it must have the kind of confrontational and militant anointing exemplified by Elijah to tear down enemy strongholds. The shell which society has erected around hearts and minds can only be penetrated "not by might, nor by power, but by my Spirit saith the Lord of hosts" (Zech. 4:6). Such an anointing is indispensable for these days. The witness of the Church "in the spirit and power of Elijah" will be far more than mere verbiage. It will be with "demonstration of the Spirit and of power" (I Cor. 2:4).

We cannot contest against the myriad of false prophets who are deceiving millions into a false antichrist religion without an "Elijah anointing." This special anointing of the Holy Spirit will visibly demonstrate the reality of the mighty God of Glory. It will convince multitudes, as it did in Elijah's time, that "the Lord, He is God!"

This supernatural empowerment enables the witness of the Church to restrain all antichrist influences until the call is issued for us to "come up higher." There is no Scripture recorded in the prophetic passages of the Bible which picture the Church as hopelessly standing by while antichrist forces bulldoze their way to world control. God's people are not without resources in these trying times. The authority which Jesus delegated the redeemed is intended to make us "more than conquerors." The Word of God affirms that believers are temples of the Holy Ghost, which means we are power houses of faith, and from our innermost being will flow a divine current capable of sweeping away the forces of darkness.

The evil of our day is not sufficient to bring the Church to a standstill. Jesus said, "Behold, I give unto you power to tread on serpents and scorpions, and over all the power of the enemy: and nothing shall by any means hurt you" (Luke 10:19).

Just as Elijah stepped up to the challenge and spoke the Word of the Lord which altered the course of a backslidden nation, the Holy Ghost is fielding a remnant who have not bowed their knee to modern Baalism. The anointed remnant will speak with authority to "principalities and powers" and break their hold on these times.

The Word of God promises "times of restitution

(restoration) of all things" just before Jesus appears in the Heavens (Acts 3:21). The believer should expect a deluge of the ██████████████████ James 5:7) at a time when gross darkness covers the people (Isa. 60:2).

It will take an "Elijah anointing" to accomplish all that God has ordained for these Last Days. The Elijah anointing disturbs the status quo and is prophesied to come "before the great and dreadful day of the Lord."

A great and dreadful day of unavoidable judgment is near, and the Lord has ordained an Elijah-type anointing to be released on His Church in these evil times. He will empower the remnant believers to issue the final warning and boldly call out for an apathetic generation to "flee the wrath that's coming."

Continue reading for further insight.

CHAPTER 2

The Spirit and Power of Elijah

*Behold, I will send you Elijah the prophet before
the coming of the great and dreadful day of the
Lord:*

Mal. 4:5

T he final words of the Old Testament comprise a
prophecy concerning the reappearance of a prophet
of God who has never died. Elijah's ministry is not finished. The Lord sent a heavenly chariot and a whirlwind
to transport him to Heaven centuries ago. He has been
waiting for the day ever since when he will return to
complete his ministry during the first half of the coming
seven years of Tribulation.

The Apostle John calls him one of the two witnesses
who will defy the antichrist and his new world order and
one-world religion. It is written in Revelation 11:3, "And
I will give power unto my two witnesses, and they shall
prophesy a thousand two hundred and threescore days,
clothed in sackcloth…" And also in Revelation 11:6,
"These have power to shut heaven, that it rain not in

the days of their prophecy: and have power over waters to turn them to blood, and to smite the earth with all plagues, as often as they will."

Many believe that the other witness will be Moses since he appeared with Elijah on the Mount of Transfiguration before the Lord's crucifixion. Some believe the other witness will be Enoch, but the prophecy in Malachi definitely identifies Elijah by name as one of the special ambassadors sent to bear witness of the truth at a time when the entire world will embrace a lie.

The prophetic Scriptures identifies the last half of the Tribulation as "the great and dreadful day of the Lord." Elijah will appear in Israel and "turn the heart of the fathers to the children, and the heart of the children to their fathers" before those final years (Mal. 4:6). This passage in Malachi reveals that Elijah's anointed ministry will reach two generations. The fathers who had abandoned the real Faith and the children who were ignorant of the Truth will both be impacted.

The anointing of the Holy Ghost on Elijah will change the hearts of blind, rebellious Jews and bring them back to the one true God of Israel. One hundred forty-four thousand (12,000 from each tribe) will recognize and accept the Lord Jesus as the Messiah, be filled with the Holy Ghost, and become flaming evangelists until God supernaturally removes them from the earth.

They will minister as a direct result of the spirit and power of Elijah. They will also defy the philosophies, policies, and practices of antichrist. They will not be just converts, but witnesses, as Elijah was a witness to his generation.

The final words in Malachi reveal a pattern that God established long ago in furthering His prophetic plan. Before He unleashes unprecedented catastrophes, or permits a time of great and dreadful judgment on civilizations and nations, He will first raise up a witness to issue one final call to repent. The prayer of Habakkuk (Hab. 3:) reveals that even "in wrath," the Lord remembers "mercy." The Apostle Peter underscored that He is "longsuffering to us-ward, not willing that any should perish, but that all should come to repentance" (II Pet. 3:9). The Lord always gives ample time and opportunity for individuals and nations to turn around so they can avoid the curses that bring judgment (Rev. 2:21).

God gives a strategic space of time for people to make decisions which will affect them for Eternity. The Holy Ghost brings conviction and repeatedly attempts to awaken people to the consequences of their sinful deeds and attitudes. The Spirit of God brings a sense of urgency in those fleeting moments to alert people of the danger that awaits them if they fail to surrender all to Jesus.

He said, "...my Spirit shall not always strive with

man" (Gen. 6:3).

As times become more serious, the need to impress upon people that the world is now in a late hour becomes more urgent. There are special anointings of the Holy Ghost released on God's messengers during the prelude of judgment. They will sound an alarm and put current events in prophetic perspective. The entire purpose of their ministry is to awaken people to their need of returning to the abandoned and rejected Faith. The Scripture reveals that God "will finish the work and cut it short in righteousness: because a short work will the Lord make upon the earth" (Rom. 9:28).

During that short period of time when unprecedented upheaval looms on the horizon, anointed servants of God are sent with "the spirit and power of Elijah" to call people out of darkness to the marvelous light.

The present condition of our world substantiates that the earth is on the fast track to unprecedented disaster. John the Baptist recognized the judgment that was approaching his generation and pled with the people to "flee the wrath to come." There are anointed voices in this perilous hour issuing the same warning and making the same appeal.

Unprecedented judgment came on the Jews just four decades after the Lord's crucifixion and resurrection. Their capital city was destroyed. Their nation was obliterated. The Jews were scattered throughout the earth for 19 centuries. Over a million were crucified by the sadistic Romans until no trees were left in the land to build any more crosses. The suffering was intolerable. All of it was avoidable if they had just recognized the time of their visitation.

America's time of visitation is rapidly coming to an end. Disaster looms on all fronts. Megadroughts in the southwest, an unprecedented heat wave in the northwest, raging crime in the major cities, an invasion of illegals on the southern border, escalating drug and human trafficking, unexpected economic instability, new threats from China, Russia, Iran, and North Korea, plus predictions of yet another lethal virus are like a tightening noose around our neck.

It is only the undeserved mercy of God that keeps our country from being overrun by our implacable enemies. The internal problems are even more serious as the plots of neo-communists push our nation toward civil war. The Spirit-filled Church cannot remain silent in such times. It is urgent that the message of salvation through repentance and faith toward God be heralded with all dispatch. A great and dreadful day is coming. The remnant believers must rise up now in the "spirit and power" of Elijah to awaken our nation to the encroaching destruction which is just ahead.

The Lord prophesied Jerusalem's destruction and the holocaust that followed in Luke 19:43-44. The Lord wept over the fate of Jerusalem for their unbelief and said, "For the days shall come upon thee, that thine enemies shall cast a trench about thee, and compass thee round, and keep thee in on every side, and shall lay thee even with the ground, and thy children within thee..."

After the Lord's resurrection, and just before His ascension, He impressed on the disciples their need to labor while it is day because night was coming when no man can work (John 9:4). The baptism in the Holy Ghost would enable them to endure and overcome the approaching upheaval. The prophetic warning Jesus spoke over Jerusalem was soon to happen, and the disciples were convinced that their world was about to be turned upside down. The disciples understood that time was of the essence – every day was important – the countdown to disaster had started – every moment was precious – the clock was ticking down to the moment when Jerusalem would be destroyed and their Temple demolished.

There was a great and dreadful day of the Lord coming. Unprecedented catastrophes would fall on that generation, and before it happened, a mighty baptism of power was needed to get people prepared. This is the reason that John the Baptist was sent as a forerunner of the Lord: "And he shall go before him in the spirit and power of Elias, to turn the hearts of the fathers to the children, and the disobedient to the wisdom of the just;

to make ready a people prepared for the Lord" (Luke 1:17). (The New Testament was written in Greek and the Old Testament was written in Hebrew. Luke uses the Greek rendition of Elijah's name in his narrative.) John the Baptist did more than minister in the style and mindset of Elijah, his message carried the same irrefutable truth to unsettle the status quo as did Elijah.

John the Baptist was not Elijah, but he ministered in the same attitude and anointing of that Old Testament prophet. Just like Elijah stood up to Ahab and Jezebel, John stood up to wicked King Herod and the crooked religious officials of his day. Just like Elijah called the nation to repentance, John baptized his hearers in the Jordan for the remission of sins. Just like Elijah confronted the evil of his time, John defied the hypocrisy, corruption, and empty religion of his day. His mission was to prepare the hearts of the people for the coming Messiah. John was a witness, like Elijah was a witness, and both proclaimed the same challenge to awaken people from their spiritual slumber.

In this day when the entire world is on the brink of unprecedented catastrophes – when every moment is precious – when the need to turn things around has never been as urgent – God has ordained the Body of Christ to be His "witnesses" in these last days. It is too late to be passive, inactive and indifferent. We are at midnight on the prophetic clock, and at midnight the cry is made, "...Behold, the bridegroom cometh; go ye out to meet Him" (Matt. 25:6). The reason Jesus emphasized the need to be baptized in the Holy Ghost was so believers could receive power to stir people from the stupor of a world caught in the throes of deception (Acts 1:8).

It is too late for the status quo of nominal Christianity which has lulled multitudes into a deep spiritual slumber. It is too late to merely go through the motions of religiosity and close our eyes to the alarming prophetic signs of the time. It is too late for a Sunday morning lecture about unimportant topics which neither edify nor inspire. It is too late for preachers to act like pop psychologists and make intellectual arguments that justify sin. Once the pulpits flame with "the spirit and power of Elijah," revival will no longer be a distant memory but a living reality.

The unique spiritual, moral, and political dangers of this time demand more than a spiritual cheerleader or a life coach. The crying need of this dark hour is for true Holy Ghost, fire-baptized witnesses to step forward with a clear word from the Lord.

Jesus said we shall do more than merely witness; He said we shall be witnesses. To be His witness is to live in the power of His Spirit and overcome the deadly evil of our time. To be His witness is to be "an example of the believer." To be His witness is to be a light in a dark place. To be His witness is to be "holy even as He is holy." To be His witness is to be salt that doesn't lose its saltiness and be a light that is not dimmed by cultural trends. To be His witness is to daily deny ourselves and take up His cross and follow Him. To be His witness is to be Heaven's ambassador in a condemned world. To be His witness is to "pray the effectual fervent prayer of a righteous man." To be His witness is to be fishers of men and laborers in His field. To be His witness is to release His power over all the power of the enemy. To be His witness is to be empowered by His Spirit to cast out devils, speak with new tongues, take up serpents, and lay hands on the sick and they shall recover.

The Greek word translated "witnesses" is *martys*, or martyr. Our modern usage of the term "martyr" refers to someone who gives their life for a cause, but the Biblical word goes much deeper. The Greek word means "one who doesn't forget and can tell what he remembers." It actually means a person who is "living proof of something . . . a person who has a personal testimony of events and relations . . .someone who boldly comes forward as a witness to confirm facts and truths."

A witness in the Biblical sense is a person who can evidence that they have direct knowledge of the Lord Jesus and display a convincing understanding of future events. A witness is willing to live and die for what he knows is right.

Since we are living in the times that Jesus described as "the beginning of sorrows," we need a special anointing of the Holy Ghost to be such a witness. These urgent times call for the measure of divine anointing that is equal to the power manifested on Elijah, because all the conditions foretold to happen during the future Tribulation are increasingly appearing. The march toward the New World Order continues unabated. High tech is taking the world into the prophesied mark of the beast. The four major sins of Tribulation times (listed in Revelation 9:20) already define the present culture: "Neither repented they of their murders (abortion), nor of their sorceries (drugs), nor of their fornication (sexual perversion), nor of their thefts (corruption)."

The one bright spot in the coming Tribulation is the ministry of the two witnesses. The spirit and the power of Elijah will be in full operation during those momentous years. Elijah is not yet on the world stage, but his time is extremely close. Since every spiritual, emotional, economic, religious, cultural, military, and political characteristic of the Tribulation is already emerging, we should expect the spirit and power of Elijah to be manifested as well.

The Spirit that empowers Elijah to "turn the hearts of the fathers to the children" is beginning to appear on the earth again. God will continue His pattern of sending special anointings of the Holy Ghost before great and dreadful days of the Lord descend.

It should be noticed that out of all the prophets and mighty men and women of God in Scripture, the only prophet whose spirit and anointing could rest on someone else was Elijah's. We do not read of the spirit of Moses, spirit of Daniel, or the spirit of Isaiah resting on anyone else, but the spirit and power of Elijah shows up just before times of unprecedented upheaval. After Elisha saw Elijah go up to Heaven in a whirlwind, the sons of the prophets recognized, "the spirit of Elijah doth rest on Elisha" (II Kings 2:15). John the Baptist, centuries later, functioned as the forerunner of Jesus in "the spirit and the power of Elijah." Now, as we face the same political, cultural, and religious attacks that confronted both Elijah and John, we should expect God to once more release powerful manifestations of His Spirit which will totally disrupt the status quo. He will not depart from the pattern foretold in Malachi's prophecy.

Look at the conditions that bring the Elijah anointing. Elijah appeared at a time when political correctness and cancel culture emerged to replace the worship of the one true God. Ahab and Jezebel, the king and Phoenician queen of Israel, made it a national policy to obliterate the worship of the God of Abraham and compel Israel to worship the heathen god Baal. The Scripture records, "And Ahab made a grove; and Ahab did more to provoke the Lord God of Israel to anger than all the kings of

Israel that were before him" (I Kings 16:33).

Ahab put unprecedented pressure on his entire nation to turn from Jehovah. He especially targeted those who were resolved to remain true to the Lord.

The prophets of God were executed or forced to hide in caves. Worship went underground. It was forbidden to worship and serve the true and living God. His Name was not to be spoken in public. His Word was denigrated and ignored. The law of God was forgotten and replaced with the warped ideas of men.

Worship is more than an acknowledgement of who God is. The Biblical concept of worship is total commitment and complete obedience to the will of the Lord as revealed in His Word. Worship doesn't begin and end in the church house. The sanctuary is where worshippers gather, but real worship is a 24/7 proposition.

Worship is not what we do; it is who we are. We are worshippers. Jesus made it clear that God would by-pass ritualistic religion and conduct a worldwide search for true worshippers. It is stated in John 4:23, "But the hour cometh, and now is, when the true worshippers shall worship the Father in spirit and in truth: for the Father seeketh such to worship him." Worship is not an event or an occasion. It's far more than a church service that begins with a song and ends with a prayer. Worship is a state of existence. It is living in a spiritual dimension that the world knows nothing about. It's a lifestyle. It's a mindset. It's how the believer lives. The Apostle Paul gave the true definition of worship in Romans 12:1-2: "I beseech you therefore, brethren, by the mercies of God, that ye present your bodies a living sacrifice, holy, acceptable unto God, which is your reasonable service. [*In the original language, the phrase "reasonable service" actually means "your most spiritual worship"*]. And be not conformed to this world: but be ye transformed by the renewing of your mind, that ye may prove what is that good, and acceptable, and perfect, will of God."

Real worship has a transforming effect on the worshipper. Our "most spiritual worship" is to offer ourselves as a living sacrifice to God. Through the renewing of our mind the worshipper will experience "the good, acceptable, and perfect will of God."

Elijah was raised up as a witness to defy and contest the evil political and religious system of Baal worship. The worship of Baal was the most blasphemous, licentious, murderous, brutal, and vicious exercise of evil that has ever existed. The name "baal" means "owner, master, husband, lord." The meaning of the name "Baal" reveals the devil's intention to completely control all the different aspects of life. The archenemy of our soul is on a quest to own and destroy everything. He plans to marry humanity to his destructive will.

The worship of Baal was actually nature worship, a kind of environmentalism, which acknowledged Baal as the supreme god of weather and climate. Ancient people named their towns and cities after the local Baals. Baal was the generic name of territorial spirits that ruled over specific localities. There was Baal Berith, Baal-Gad, Baal-Haron, Baal-Hermon, and so forth. Baal was tied to the economy of those places because this false god was thought to determine rainfall. Baalism was the merger of nature worship with the economy and was celebrated with sexual orgies and human sacrifice.

The "high places" mentioned in the Scripture were scenes of grotesque immorality. Children were sacrificed on the altars of Baal. The image of Baal had brass hands that were heated white hot. Then babies were placed on those hands and burned alive. The priests and worshippers of Baal would dance and yell so vociferously that the screams of the babies could not be heard. They watched as the skins of the children burned and shriveled under intense heat. They paid special attention to the mouth of the child because the contraction of the skin made those innocent infants appear to be laughing in the last agonizing seconds of their lives. In the detestably warped thinking of Baal worshippers, the child laughed himself to death. Sexual perversion and self-mutilation were an intricate part of these rituals. The Baal worshippers would eat human flesh in these celebrations. We get the word "cannibalism" from the practices of Baal worship.

Baal worship was the epitome of satanic activity.

For this reason, Jesus called satan, "Baal Zebub" or "lord of the flies, master of the dung pile, the owner and originator of every disease-carrying pest." Words fail to describe the disgusting tendency of the Israelites who broke their covenant with the true God and turned to the repulsive, degrading, diabolic worship of Baal.

Elijah came forward to do more than denounce the evil of this cancel culture. He announced, "As the Lord God of Israel liveth, before whom I stand, there shall not be dew nor rain these years, but according to my word" (I Kings 17:1). Most people don't realize what Elijah was doing at this point. He wasn't capriciously speaking from his own heart or mind. He was repeating a stipulation in Israel's covenant with God. There was a provision of the covenant that had been conveniently overlooked by the people. It was a warning ignored and mocked by their rulers. The Law of God stated in Deuteronomy 11:16-17, "Take heed to yourselves, that your heart be not deceived, and ye turn aside, and serve other gods, and worship them; And then the Lord's wrath be kindled against you, and he shut up the heaven, that there be no rain, and that the land yield not her fruit; and lest ye perish quickly from off the good land which the Lord giveth you."

Israel was in violation of God's command and not deserving of its annual rainfall. Elijah took God's Word and deployed it as a weapon to challenge the prevailing culture. The people were convinced that their "climate change" idol was the rain maker and was appeased by their debauchery. The entire nation was content to believe a lie, but then Elijah stepped forward with the eternal Word of the living God, and informed a generation obsessed with abominations that they were about to be shaken into reality by the real rain maker. He was bold enough to speak at a time when most were convinced the law of God was no longer relevant, no longer true, and no longer in control. Elijah was a witness to the Truth and exposed the lie they were living under.

The Word is always true, relevant, and powerful enough to change conditions and circumstances. However, there is a condition that must be met to make the Word of God effective. The Word must be spoken to have an impact. The Roman centurion understood this principle. He said to Jesus, "Speak the Word only, and my servant will be healed" (Matt. 8:8). The Word must have a voice. The promises of God are voice-activated. Somebody with Holy Ghost boldness must stand up and speak it or nothing will ever change.

Baalism is here again. It is the new religion in America. Today it is called "wokeism." A columnist for the *New York Magazine* recently wrote, "We have the cult of social justice on the left…a religion whose followers show the same zeal as any born again Evangelical."[1]

---

1 Andrew Sullivan, "America's New Religions," *New York Magazine*, 7

Linguist John McWhorter wrote in *The Atlantic,* "Antiracism is a profoundly religious movement in everything but terminology."[2]

Everything from politics, sports, corporations, education, and even religious denominations have embraced the new Baalism. Some psychologists are warning that wokeism qualifies as a mental disorder because of the insane changes its followers are forcing on the country.

At the heart of wokeness is racial hatred. It scapegoats all whites as irredeemable racists who must be punished because of the color of their skin. The Oregon Department of Education issued a statement that "math is racist because it requires a correct answer."[3] These educators claim that math is really a disguised form of white supremacy. In New York City, math education professor Laurie Rubel claims the whole notion that $2 + 2 = 4$ "reeks of white supremacist patriarchy."[4] A Brooklyn College professor stated, "the idea that math or data is

December 2018.

2 John McWhorter, "The Virtue Signalers Won't Change the World," *The Atlantic,* 23 December 2018.

3 Kipp Jones, "Oregon Pushes Idea That Math Is Racist, Encourages Teachers to Dismantle White Supremacy," *The Western Journal,* 12 February 2021.

4 Emma Colton, "Math Professor Claims Equation 2+2=4 'Reeks of White Supremacist Patriarchy," *The Washington Examiner,* 10 August 2020.

culturally neutral or in any way objective is a myth."[5] The State Education Department of Oregon now has a curriculum called "The Pathway to Math Equity." It tells public school teachers how to use mathematics to "dismantle racism." The teacher's guide says, "The concept of mathematics being purely objective is unequivocally false." The insane assertions of this hateful teacher's manual are that "upholding the ideas that there are always right and wrong answers perpetuate objectivity as well as fear of open conflict. We see white supremacy culture showing up in the mathematics classroom even as we carry out our professional responsibilities."[6]

This lunacy would be laughable if it weren't so tragic. These lunatics are not on the fringe of society anymore. They now control the institutions that define the culture. It was reported by the *Washington Free Beacon* on July 24, 2020, that Rutgers University recently determined that speaking and writing English correctly is – just like math – totally racist. The report stated that the school's English department is altering its grammar standards to "stand with and respond" to the Black Lives Matter movement and emphasize "critical

---

5 Tom Ciccotta, "Brooklyn College Education Prof. Claims Math is 'White Supremacist Patriarchy,'" Breitbart.com, 10 August 2020.

6 Kipp Jones, "Oregon Pushes Idea That Math Is Racist, Encourages Teachers to Dismantle White Supremacy," *The Western Journal*, 12 February 2021.

grammar" over "irrelevancies" like correct spelling and proper grammar.[7] After a considerable amount of criticism, the school denied these remarks.

The California State Board of Education recently voted to make "woke" curriculum mandatory for its public school graduates. The curriculum says that the pilgrims committed "theocide" in destroying the belief in traditional Aztec gods with the teachings of Christianity.[8] The curriculum teaches that it's the duty of students to revive the worship of these ancient gods and undo the damage that Christianity has done. Lessons are complete with chants and prayers to these gods, some of whom were worshipped with human sacrifice. Students will be taught to call on these gods for a "revolutionary spirit" that will bring "liberation, transformation, and decolonization."

Ten years ago, no one would have believed that a time would come in America when children would be taught to pray to demons in public school. Yet the unthinkable is happening.

Wokeism is also being promoted by corporations and businesses. A prominent nationwide chain store is

7 Chrissy Clark, "Rutgers Declares Grammar Racist," *Washington Free Beacon*, 24 July 2020.

8 Cameron Hildtich, "California Curriculum Accuses Christians of 'Theocide,' Encourages Chanting to Pagan Gods," nationalreview. com, 16 March 2021.

selling a video prayer book, written by a person with a doctorate degree, in which she begs her god to help her "hate white people." Most of this wokeism is not really about social justice or white supremacy. Those issues are just a cover for the real intent of wokeism which is to destroy Bible Christianity and replace the Faith of our Fathers with godless Marxism.

Wokeism in every sense is a replacement religion for Bible Truth. Its sacred texts are the *Communist Manifesto* and a book published in 2001 called *Critical Race Theory*. Its main doctrines are cultural and ethnic division. It has a number of prophets who are continually writing books and leading diversity training sessions in government and throughout the private sector. It has its identifying terms. Bible believers know the meaning of Scriptural terms such as propitiation, justification, and substitutionary atonement. Wokeism also has its identifying terms which are diversity, inclusion, and equity. Its core doctrines are hatred for whites, intersectionality, microaggression, and systemic racism.

This new religion advocates violence and forced conversions. The adherents of this demented philosophy condemn in the harshest terms anyone who will not repeat their slogans, march in their protests, or agree with their ideas. If you don't agree with them, you have committed the "unpardonable" and are branded a racist, a bigot, and prejudiced. Those who refuse to submit to their creed must be fired from their jobs, ostracized by their communities, and publicly shamed. It is the goal of the "woke" advocates to punish their opposition legally, financially, and expel them from society.

This new religion is intolerant and refuses to co-exist with anything else. This new Baalism compels its followers to tear down monuments, censor children's cartoons, burn American flags, defund the police, and destroy cities. This new religion has their chants and mass religious meetings. They call them "protests." It also requires confessions and kneeling. The Speaker of the House of Representatives, Nancy Pelosi, recently led Democratic congressmen in a kneeling session to bow to this new religion of wokeness. Whiteness is their unpardonable sin. The only thing this new religion lacks is their false Christ, but rest assured, he is on the way.

The nation is so deep into this new Baal worship that the media is openly boasting about America's new godlessness. An article in the *Los Angeles Times* was recently headlined, "Why America's Record Godlessness is Good News for the Nation." The article read, "The secularization of US society—the waning of religious faith, practice, and affiliation—is continuing at a dramatic and historically unprecedented pace. While many consider such a development as a cause for concern, such a worry is not warranted. This increasing godlessness in America is actually a good thing, to be welcomed and embraced."[9]

Anyone who dares to research this cultural phenomenon will discover that wokeness has brought our country record-breaking crime, unprecedented drug use, terminal overdoses, and unprecedented racial division. It has destroyed the health care system, turned schools into indoctrination centers, ended our national sovereignty, and unleashed unparalleled perversion on the land. It is incredulous to think that the media said "this is a good thing." God's indictment on a country that embraces such manifestations of Baalism is recorded in Isaiah 5:20-24:

> [20] Woe unto them that call evil good, and good evil; that put darkness for light, and light for darkness; that put bitter for sweet, and sweet for bitter!
>
> [21] Woe unto them that are wise in their own eyes, and prudent in their own sight!
>
> [22] Woe unto them that are mighty to drink wine, and men of strength to mingle strong drink:
>
> [23] Which justify the wicked for reward, and take away the righteousness of the righteous

9 Phil Zuckerman, "Op-Ed: Why America's record godlessness is good news for the nation," *Los Angeles Times*, April 2, 2021.

from him!

[24] Therefore as the fire devoureth the stubble, and the flame consumeth the chaff, so their root shall be as rottenness, and their blossom shall go up as dust: because they have cast away the law of the LORD of hosts, and despised the word of the Holy One of Israel.

It is imperative that the Blood-bought Church of Jesus Christ have the spirit and power of Elijah to oppose these merchants of evil. The "spirit and power of Elijah" is a confrontational anointing that destroys passive attitudes and complacency. It is a bold anointing that doesn't hesitate, doesn't compromise, doesn't cave in, and doesn't back down. It is a no-nonsense anointing that doesn't negotiate with sin. It is the anointing that repairs the broken altar of God. It is the anointing that exhibits unswerving faith in God's power to answer prayer.

Elijah baptized the restored altar of God with 12 barrels of sea water, yet heavenly fire still flamed upon it. The "spirit and power of Elijah" is the anointing that calls fire down from Heaven on impossible situations. Water-logged sacrifices don't burn except on altars repaired by someone with the Spirit of the Lord upon them. The prime attribute of the "spirit and the power of Elijah" is a tenacious anointing that won't give up.

The issue on Mt. Carmel as Elijah opposed the prophets of Baal was, "Who is the real rain maker? Who can end the drought? Who can stop the famine?" The bold challenge to Israel was, "How long halt ye between two opinions? if the Lord be God, follow him: but if Baal, then follow him...the God that answers by fire, let Him be God!" (I Kings 18:21).

After the fire fell and the prophets of Baal lay slain before the altar of God, Elijah heard the sound of an abundance of rain which no one else could hear. He actually heard the literal sound of rain. It wasn't hyperbole. It wasn't hype. It was a real sound. He heard the sound when there wasn't anything to see . . .no cloud . . .no mist . . . nothing on the horizon. There was only the sound of rain which no one had heard for three long years.

The believers who are sensitive to the Spirit of God in these Endtimes will not look at the things which are seen, but at the things which are not seen (II Cor. 4:18). The sound of an abundance of rain can still be heard by those with ears to hear (Matt. 13:9). The ability to spiritually discern the coming activity of the Holy Ghost is characteristic of the spirit of Elijah, and God is moving once again.

It wasn't until Elijah took the sword and destroyed the prophets of Baal that he heard the sound which announced the long drought was ending. The Scripture affirms that the weapons of our warfare are not carnal. We have offensive weapons that will pull down enemy strongholds. It takes the anointing of the Holy Ghost for our weapons to be effective. It takes divine intervention to hear "what the Spirit is saying to the church." God will speak clearly when in the Name of Jesus we take the sharp sword of the Spirit, the Word of God, and silence the influences of Baal.

When the entire system of Baal worship is destroyed individually, locally, or nationally, then an apparent insignificant cloud will arise, rapidly expand, and drench a dry and thirsty land with rain. When Baal is overturned in an individual's personal life, the long spiritual and financial drought will be over, and God will show up with showers of blessings. It is then that the believer will hear the sound of "the former and the later rain" coming upon the earth.

The anointing of the Holy Ghost, ordained for God's people in these critical times, will come in the Elijah mode. Intercessors will call fire down from Heaven to defeat the false gods of the culture and turn a generation to Biblical Truth.

Oh, Lord, let the fire fall again in a way that will convince this confused and frustrated nation that you alone are God!

CHAPTER 3
Where is the Lord God of Elijah?

And he took the mantle of Elijah that fell from him, and smote the waters, and said, Where is the Lord God of Elijah? and when he also had smitten the waters, they parted hither and thither: and Elisha went over.

II Kings 2:14

It has been repeatedly stated that these are perilous times. The dangers of these times are gaining the attention of practically every segment of the population. It should be evident to all that our nation is at the beginning of a civil war where communists and patriots will eventually clash in mortal combat.

General McInerny, a three-star general, formerly the head of military intelligence, recently documented the foreign involvement in the 2020 election and said there is no question that World War III has already begun. He said that unlike the wars of the past, this war is first being fought in cyberspace as high-tech companies in league with foreign powers exert their totalitarian will on a vulnerable nation.

Early in 2021, the ~~entire world~~ watched in stunned amazement as ~~████████████~~ became an armed camp. Politicians whipped up hysteria against a perceived, but non-existent, threat claiming that conservatives were planning an attack on the incoming regime. At the height of the fictitious insurrection scare, there were more troops in Washington, D.C. than the U.S. armed forces stationed in Afghanistan. The infamous Deep State with their media allies pushed the narrative that conservatives and Christians were actually insurrectionists who were plotting to overthrow the government.

The new administration has labeled Bible-believing Christians "domestic terrorists." The hatred of the regime for Bible Christians was expressed by the CEO of the government-funded PBS network in a bellicose statement which should alarm all freedom-loving Americans. He openly stated that the children of conservative Christians should be taken from their parents and put in re-education camps. Other high-level voices are jumping on the bandwagon to initiate a new period of persecution against Bible believers. The Chairman of Homeland Security suggested that supporters of the former president be put on a no-fly list. Congresswoman Ocasio-Cortez advocated that all conservatives be registered in the same manner that sex offenders are registered. One congressman used the "n" word to describe conservatives and said that "this is how they should be treated."

The dominance of the current woke ideology is destroying history, heritage, and patriotism. One Democratic representative seriously considered introducing a bill to scrap the national anthem. The "woke" advocates are even claiming that the American flag is racist and must be redesigned. The momentum to destroy our history by eliminating our Judeo-Christian heritage has gone into high gear. The public statements of politicians and bureaucrats reveal that they are convinced America cannot be "fundamentally changed" until committed Bible Christians are somehow removed.

This new woke-driven persecution against Christians is happening at a time when our mortal enemies—Iran, China, and North Korea—are plotting new attacks on the homeland. The dictator of North Korea senses the weakness of a new administration and vows to double down on his nuclear program to eventually attack the United States. Iran recently boasted that they will destroy Israel in the next two decades and promised a retaliatory strike on the US to avenge the death of its top general. China celebrated the inauguration of the new administration with a statement which said China can now do anything it wants over the entire earth.

Everyone from Franklin Graham to Dr. Dobson to a Vatican Archbishop is predicting tough times for all Christians under the new administration. The new regime will continue to use the covid pandemic as an excuse to harass churches. Some government agencies are advocating removing the tax-exempt status of churches if they do not change their doctrine to endorse the LGBTQ agenda. Public schools across the nation are implementing new curriculums which praise Marxism while denigrating the nation's free enterprise system. The true history of our nation is being erased, and the next generation is being taught to hate the ideas of our founding fathers and regard America as a hopelessly incorrigible country. If trends continue, America will soon look like South Africa or Venezuela in the next few years.

It is an understatement to say that our nation is in turmoil, hopelessly divided, and threatened with a totalitarian communist dictatorship. The country once prided itself as being "the land of the free and the home of the brave," but is now in a pitiful, surreal, and bizarre condition. People are in a daze, hoping that someone will awaken us from this nightmare. But our present reality is not just a bad dream that passes in the morning light. The rapid collapse of our country is happening in real time. America is witnessing an avalanche of executive orders and institutional corruption which threatens to destroy all of our constitutional rights and freedom.

The believers are left wondering, "What happened

to America?" The unspoken questions have started to be uttered: "Has God forsaken us? . . . Why did He allow this to happen? . . .What about all the prophecies that foretold a different result in the presidential election? . . .Didn't the Lord hear our prayer? . . .Has He surrendered the country to judgment? . . .Will we have any freedom left after the demolition job of the new administration is finished? . . .What do we do now?"

Such questions demand an answer, but there is no simple answer that can be given. It must first be acknowledged that the day is quickly coming when America will experience the righteous judgment of God on a scale it has never known. No nation has been permitted to exist who slaughtered the innocent, embraced perversion, blasphemed God, turned to idolatry, persecuted believers, and fell to the depths of moral depravity which is now mainstream in America.

Second Kings 17:8-17 is a passage enshrined in the Scriptures as a warning to all nations who callously follow the downward path of ancient Israel. This rather lengthy list of indictments clearly spells out the certainty of judgment for those nations who are guilty of such crimes:

> [8] And they walked in the statutes of the heathen . . .
>
> [9] And the children of Israel did secretly those

things that were not right against the Lord their God . . .

[10] And they set them up images and groves. . . [orgies and places to sacrifice their children].

[11] . . . and wrought wicked things to provoke the Lord to anger:

[13] Yet the Lord testified against Israel, and against Judah, by all the prophets, and by all the seers, saying, Turn ye from your evil ways, and keep my commandments and my statutes, according to all the law which I commanded your fathers . . .

[14] Notwithstanding they would not hear, but hardened their necks . . .

[15] And they rejected his statutes, and his covenant . . . and went after the heathen that were round about them, concerning whom the Lord had charged them, that they should not do like them.

[16] And they left all the commandments of the Lord their God . . . and served Baal.

[17] And they caused their sons and their daughters to pass through the fire, and used divination and enchantments, and sold themselves to do evil in the sight of the Lord, to provoke

him to anger.

The Holy Spirit continued the charges against Israel in Second Chronicles 36:16, ". . . they mocked the messengers of God, and despised his words, and misused his prophets, until the wrath of the Lord arose against his people, till there was no remedy." The Psalmist summarized the downward spiral of any nation that departs from the precepts and truth of God in Psalm 106:15, "And He gave them their request; but sent leanness into their soul." America is now guilty of all the charges in the divine indictment.

However, the Lord never releases wrath on any nation without first providing a way of escape. Noah was told to build an Ark. Lot was forced out of wicked Sodom by angels. The Hebrews were exempted from the plagues on Egypt. In 70 AD, the Romans destroyed Jerusalem and obliterated Israel. They crucified over one million Jews. Yet it is historically verified that not one believer was among the victims because the Lord told the disciples to flee Jerusalem long before the calamity transpired.

Indisputable prophetic signs indicate that the world is close to Tribulation times. Jesus told us that during the lead-up to the prophesied seven years, we shall be hated of all nations for His Name's sake (Matt. 24:9). The Apostle Paul foretold that real Christians would be attacked by an ungodly society in Second Timothy 3:12:

"Yea, and all that will live godly in Christ Jesus shall suffer persecution."

However, all believers must remember the specific instructions of the Holy Ghost in response to such intense spiritual assaults and societal attacks. The way to overcome is recorded in First Peter 4:14, 16: "If ye be reproached for the name of Christ, happy are ye; for the spirit of glory and of God resteth upon you: on their part he is evil spoken of, but on your part he is glorified…if any man suffer as a Christian, let him not be ashamed; but let him glorify God on this behalf."

God will not forsake His people in times of persecution and testing. God's people can face the uncertainty and upheaval of our times with the assurance stated in Second Peter 2:9: "The Lord knoweth how to deliver the godly out of temptations, and to reserve the unjust unto the day of judgment to be punished:" The glorious Church will successfully overcome the war waged by evil men against the truth in these Last Days. The Scripture is clear that "the mystery of iniquity (lawlessness) doth already work: only he who now letteth [hinders] will let [hinder], until he be taken out of the way" (2 Thess. 2:7).

This passage refers to the Spirit-filled Church restraining the forces of darkness until the Lord forcibly removes us from this judgment-bound planet at the Rapture.

It is in times of great pressure and frustration, when we have not yet seen the visible manifestation of God's supernatural intervention, that we are tempted to question, "Where is the Lord?" The patriarch Job questioned at the height of his painful ordeal: "Where is God my maker, who giveth songs in the night;" (Job 35:10). *Night* in the Scripture is a symbol of calamity and conveys a dark time of gloom and despair. *Songs* in the Scripture are always emblematic of testimonies. The prophet Zechariah noted that even in the darkest night, God will bring forth a testimony that will illuminate the times: "…But it shall come to pass, that at evening time it shall be light" (Zech. 14:7).

Gideon was just as perplexed about the events of his day as we are about our present circumstances. When the angel informed him that the Lord was about to deliver Israel from the oppressive Midianites, Gideon responded in Judges 6:13, "…if the Lord be with us, why then is all this befallen us? and where be all his miracles which our fathers told us of…"

Gideon was hiding from his enemies, but the Lord addressed him as "a mighty man of valour." God did not speak to him as though he was a fear-struck coward. The Lord addressed him as the person he would become, not the person that he was. The Holy Ghost first works inwardly to change us into someone He can use to bring deliverance from spiritual, political, financial, and cultural bondage.

Our God still "calleth those things which be not as though they were" (Rom. 4:17). Gideon's encounter with God was transformative and changed him from a vacillating spiritual weakling into a champion of faith. The Spirit of the Lord came upon him after he built an altar and called it Jehovah-Shalom (the Lord our peace).

There is a desperate need for the neglected altar of prayer to be built again where the peace of God can once more reign in our hearts (Col. 3:15). The power and boldness to transform us into more than conquerors will not come until those commitments which have been abandoned are renewed at the altar.

Once Gideon found peace at the altar of Jehovah-Shalom, he had the courage to throw down the altar of Baal and destroy the licentious grove where evil was practiced. The altar experience started a chain reaction of victories and charted a new course for Gideon. The Spirit of the Lord came upon him and he blew the trumpet, calling the men of Israel to war.

Those who responded to the trumpet call were vetted at the water. Only those who quenched their thirst with their eyes on the prize were selected for the battle. Gideon discovered that he just needed 300 "sold out" believers to defeat a multitude of Midianites. Just 300 men with the right focus could tap into divine strategies and release the needed power to free a generation from their oppressors.

The massive army of Midian was thrown into consternation when they heard the sound of breaking vessels and saw flaming sparks illuminate the night sky. The adversaries turned on themselves when the 300 shouted, "The Sword of the Lord, and of Gideon" (Jgs. 7:20). The writer of Hebrews penned this comment about the conflict: Gideon "...escaped the edge of the sword, out of weakness was made strong, waxed valiant in fight, turned to flight the army of the aliens" (Heb. 11:34).

Through a series of miraculous victories, God answered Gideon's frustrated questions. He found that the singular reason for all the misery, calamity and disaster which befell his nation was because the altar of God had been replaced with the altar of Baal. The timeless truth learned from Gideon's episode is that once the covenant people return to Jehovah Shalom, and throw down the competing pagan altars of false gods, the multitude of oppressing enemies and problems will be totally defeated.

Gideon's complaint of "where be all the miracles" changed into a shout. He watched the enemy fall when they shouted, "The Sword of the Lord, and of Gideon." The days of miracles are not over, but we will not see the mighty manifestations of the Holy Ghost until a new surrender is made at the old-fashioned altar of repentance.

Repentance, surrender, and renouncing sin are topics which have been stricken from the lexicon of today's Christians. Prayer meetings have been replaced with endless activities which do nothing to redeem the lost or revive the Church. The true Gospel has been convoluted into a hodgepodge of pop psychology and political correctness. So many churches have gone "woke" to fit in with today's dangerously perverted culture.

The insanity of our times will get worse until a hunger for the real Presence of Jesus and a return to the "whole counsel of God" becomes the first priority of believers. The so-called seeker-sensitive approach which gives credence to the fallen morays of the culture, the false grace teachings which deceive people into believing the Lord overlooks sin and denigrates righteous living as "unnecessary works," the inclusive theology which falsely claims that all roads lead to Heaven, the new apostolic reformation movement which demeans the deity of Jesus and attempts to replace the local church with celebrity ministries, dominion theology which cancels out the promise of the Lord's Return, and the plethora of modern heresies must be "cut down" just as much as Gideon was compelled to cut down the idolatrous grove of Baal.

Once the trees of false doctrine with their toxic fruit are cut down, it will be discovered again that "the Sword of the Lord and of Gideon" is still able to do "exceedingly abundantly above all that we ask or think, according to the power that worketh in us" (Eph. 3:20).

Elisha stood on the banks of the Jordan with immense challenges facing him and questioned, "Where is the Lord God of Elijah?" Elijah's ministry was unfinished. Enemies remained. Ancient Israel witnessed fire fall from Heaven and experienced the power of God to end a megadrought that threatened their very existence . . . but they did nothing to change. The people shouted and rejoiced in a miraculous moment, but, sadly, when that moment was over, they did not repent. Such response to the mighty move of the Holy Ghost is common today.

The Israelites soon relapsed to old ways despite experiencing the mighty power and provision of God when Heavenly fire supernaturally fell and rain returned after being absent for so long. This is the experience of thousands today who have tasted the goodness of the Lord but have not reciprocated. The presence of God has been manifested in countless services and people have been touched by His power, but untold thousands refuse to respond to His Spirit by committing themselves totally to Him. There is always happiness in the things which God does to heal the sick, free the captives, restore health, relieve the oppressed, and bestow financial blessings on those who are struggling, but so many who receive such wonderful victories never break with their past. The initial euphoria of the Lord's miraculous presence soon fades and they lapse back into their old ways.

According to the Scripture, "they received…the grace of God in vain" (II Cor. 6:1).

Elisha was aware that he could not contend with the fickleness of people, or the cunning plots of Jezebel, or the enemy nations which surrounded Israel, unless he received a double portion of the anointing which rested on Elijah. The stipulation for the desired anointing was to remain with Elijah until he was taken up. Elisha had to turn down the invitations to stay at Gilgal, Bethel, Jericho, and Jordan. Determination was the driving force that kept Elisha resolved to follow the anointing until the time came for it to be transferred. He said to Elijah, "…As the Lord liveth, and as thy soul liveth, I will not leave thee…" (II Kings 2:2).

Elisha was in pursuit of an active anointing, not a stale, dormant, deflated experience. He innately knew that the anointing on Elijah was destined to remain on the earth while Elijah himself would be translated to Heaven. The anointing of the Holy Ghost is designed to remain on the earth. There is no need for the anointing in Heaven. The Spirit of God revealed to the prophet Isaiah that the anointing destroys the yoke (Isa. 10:27). The earth realm is where captive souls are in need of power that can set them free. Elisha could not be dissuaded or his focus diverted. He was determined to receive a double portion of the spirit and power of Elijah. The "spirit and the power of Elijah" is not about the personality of this Old Testament prophet, but about the exploits which God accomplished through him. Today the Lord is looking for those determined, passionate, committed believers upon whom He can manifest that same anointing again.

The prophetic promise is that the "people that do know their God shall be strong, and do exploits" (Dan. 11:32). The exploits which are needed in this last desperate hour include a sin-killing revival that turns the younger generation away from "woke" ideology, a manifestation of God's power that delivers from drugs, an awakening to the evils of a promiscuous lifestyle, and an understanding that there is only one "name under Heaven…whereby we must be saved" (Acts 4:12). The outpouring of the Spirit will deliver from the myriad cults, from socialism, from Marxism, from hateful Critical Race Theory, from violence, from suicide, from the lie of false grace, from indulging in alcohol, from sexual sin, and from every device of the ultimate deceiver who comes to "steal, kill, and destroy."

The name of the river where Elisha received the double portion experience is highly significant. The word "Jordan" means "the descender." Elisha received an answer to the whereabouts of the Lord God of Elijah at "the descender." As our nation descends into unprecedented chaos, unparalleled deception, and unmitigated evil, the "spirit and power of Elijah" will be manifested once more. Someone will take up the fallen mantle and smite the surging current of wickedness. For a short space of time, the flood of iniquity will roll back to prove to a skeptical generation that God is still God. The Lord will manifest His Glory at the descending point.

The patriarch Job put into words the conundrum of sincere hearts who long for divine intervention when he said in Job 23:

> ³ Oh that I knew where I might find him! that I might come even to his seat!
>
> ⁸ Behold, I go forward, but he is not there; and backward, but I cannot perceive him:
>
> ⁹ On the left hand, where he doth work, but I cannot behold him: he hideth himself on the right hand, that I cannot see him:
>
> ¹⁰ But he knoweth the way that I take: when he hath tried me, I shall come forth as gold.

A purified Church who refuses to compromise Biblical truth and declines to lower the standards of godly living is about to discover the answer to Elisha's longstanding question. The Lord God of Elijah will show up suddenly to roll back the tide of evil so the

Church can complete its assignment before the great and dreadful day of the Lord.

The message God sent to His people through the prophet Hosea reveals the deliverance that will come to the redeemed in times of unprecedented trouble. The prophecy recorded in Hosea 2:15 speaks of a specific valley. It is not a metaphoric location, but a literal valley experience which all covenant people will know from time to time. The Lord called the valley *Achor*, which means "trouble, tribulation, and deep sorrow."

The truth revealed in Hosea's prophecy is that dark valleys are not the ultimate destination of the people of God. The Valley of Trouble is not a place where the child of God remains for very long. The Lord said He will open a door in the Valley of Trouble. It is a door of escape. It is a door to restoration. It is a passage to greater things.

This prophetic passage reveals that in the VALLEY OF ACHOR, the Lord's transformative power will be manifested. Instead of the mournful wails of disappointment and the lamentations of defeat, God said His people "shall sing there, as in the days of her youth, and as in the day when she came up out of the land of Egypt."

The ageless Word of God in this prophecy verifies to believers that another time of deliverance is coming. Today, especially in the current oppressive turmoil, every believer has arrived at the Valley of Achor. It is an uncomfortable place where we are attacked from all sides, but we won't be stuck here. The Holy Spirit will lead us from glory to glory, not from defeat to defeat. No believer should expect to stay in the valley of trouble.

In the Valley of Achor, God promised to take the names of Baalim out of our mouth: "For I will take away the names of Baalim out of her mouth, and they shall no more be remembered by their name" (Hos. 2:17).

It seems that the most common topic of conversation in this time of uncertainty, even among believers, is the intolerable conditions that are foisted upon us. We know so well the names of our attackers and oppressors. Every day, the evil-ruling elite take new actions that make our load heavier and our burden more difficult. But the door of hope is soon to open, and we will pass through it to forget the things which are behind. The names of the false demigods who have blasphemed and mocked the God of Glory will soon fade away. The Lord will satisfy our mouth with good things and the topic of conversation will change from how bad things are to how good God is.

The evil report is about to change into a glorious testimony. Soon the common word of praise on the lips of the Blood-washed redeemed will be "what the devil meant for evil, God has turned for good."

Hosea's prophecy is an assurance that the Lord has heard the cry of people in the valley of trouble and will not let our prayer go unanswered. God is about to show up and show out. We are about to experience the mighty power of the Lord ████████████ precedented ways.

CHAPTER 4

America Needs a Baal-Out

And he said, I have been very jealous for the LORD God of hosts: because the children of Israel have forsaken thy covenant, thrown down thine altars, and slain thy prophets with the sword; and I, even I only, am left; and they seek my life, to take it away.

I Kings 19:14

In 2008, the economy of the nation was teetering on the verge of collapse. There was much talk in those days of the Great Recession. The strain on the economy was brought about by major corporations that were mismanaged and insolvent. Major layoffs were sending the unemployment rate to dangerous levels, and the crisis was causing panic in lending institutions. The banking industry was feeling the ripple effect of the growing crisis, and the value of the currency was threatened. From across the economic spectrum came cries for a government "bail out." The seeds were sown back then for more government control over business, and the socialist agenda began to surface.

Then in 2019 and through 2020, a made-to-order pandemic forced thousands of small businesses to close, and the cry for a government bail-out became loud and more vociferous. The pressure for even more and larger bail-outs resulted in an impossible national debt that soared into the stratosphere with every passing day. Even now, with a crisis on our southern border and a questionable recovery from a global pandemic, pressure is building on politicians to come up with yet another bail-out plan.

But the first two bail-outs did not work. The economic situation is now even more serious in spite of government largess. The economy has become more uncertain with plans to increase taxes that will surely bring new perils to the nation's financial structure.

Our leaders are totally blind to the fact that the economy will never be fixed as long as they lead the nation into more immorality and abominations. A moral meltdown always brings an economic meltdown. Isaiah 60:12 says, "For the nation and kingdom that will not serve thee shall perish; yea, those nations shall be utterly wasted."

Every important device comes with an owner's manual which not only explains how the apparatus functions, but also how to fix what is broken. It is ludicrous to think that the operator's manual can be thrown away and then expect things to go well. Yet that's exactly what this country has done in rejecting the Word of God. No matter how often the atheists, socialists, and Marxists deny that this nation was founded on the principles of God's Word, it is a matter of historical record that the founders deliberately based our institutions on the standards of right and wrong taught in the Scriptures. Those founders of long ago believed "righteousness exalteth a nation: but sin is a reproach to any people" (Prov. 14:34).

The prophet Isaiah spoke prophetically of the conditions that now envelop the leadership of our land: "Woe unto them that decree unrighteous decrees [unjust laws], and that write grievousness [the Hebrew word is 'amal' meaning wickedness] which they have prescribed: To turn aside the needy from judgment, and to take away the right of the poor of my people . . . And what will ye do in the day of visitation [the Hebrew word is 'pequddah' meaning inspection that causes a change in circumstances], and in the desolation [the Hebrew word is 'sho'ah' which means utter devastation] which shall come from far? to whom will ye flee for help? and where will ye leave your glory?" (Isa. 10:1-3).

The implication of this verse is that the proud, arrogant leaders who denigrated Biblical directives will suddenly find themselves at a total loss. The prophet Isaiah's questions to those leaders who factored God out of national life is an indictment on their belligerence and hostility to His Word. A day of reckoning is fast approaching. Who will they turn to for help when the "great reset" becomes "the great collapse"?

Early in the Psalms, David revealed the calamity which envelops those who rage against God: "The kings of the earth set themselves, and the rulers take counsel together, against the LORD, and against his anointed, saying, Let us break their bands asunder, and cast away their cords from us. He that sitteth in the heavens shall laugh: the LORD shall have them in derision. Then shall he speak unto them in his wrath, and vex them in his sore displeasure" (Psa. 2:2-5).

It seems that all of nature went into convulsions during the pandemic. There was an unprecedented number of earthquakes, massive flooding, unprecedented snowfall in the northeast, over half the country's agriculture acreage devastated by drought, a rise in the number of destructive tornadoes, and an escalation in mysterious diseases. Most of our national assets are now in the hands of foreign corporations, and a large portion of our economy is actually controlled by our enemies.

North Korea is constantly threatening a new conflict with its nuclear weapons. It appears that the lives of thousands of our soldiers and untold millions of dollars were wasted in Iraq, because just as soon as our troops pulled out, our enemy, Iran, moved in to take control. The shameful retreat of American forces in Afghanistan, turning billions of dollars of sophisticated weaponry to Taliban butchers, and unleashing genocide against Christians, is another example of America's rapid decline on the international scene. Russia has renewed the Cold War and is constantly testing our defenses with nuclear warplanes penetrating our airspace and submarines patrolling our coastlines. China continues on its path of world domination and infiltrating our nation at every level.

God is trying to tell this nation something, but no one in Washington or the White House is listening. We are in the lead-up time to the awful wrath of the coming seven years of Tribulation. Already the unrepentant attitude predicted for the final days is increasing with alarming regularity.

Our society is dominated by the four big sins listed in Revelation 9. Our culture is inundated with drugs, perversion, corruption and abortion. These are not just personal sins, but national sins that are legalized, promoted, and embraced. Our nation has reached the exponential curve of wickedness culminating in a return to the days of Noah when God said, "The earth was also corrupt before God and the earth was filled with violence…the end of all flesh is come before me" (Gen. 6:11,13). There is no future for this country if it persists on its present path to destruction.

America is in desperate need of a "Baal-out," but

it is not the bail-out which most think about. It is not a financial bail-out that is needed as much as a spiritual Baal-out! The spiritual roots of the present crisis must be examined, exposed, and rooted out, or the country envisioned by our founders will not survive.

It is ironic that as the world approaches the most horrendous seven years of its history, there is renewed interest among the ruling elite in all things pertaining to the vile idolatry of Baal. Just before the pandemic hit, World Heritage, an organization under the auspices of UNESCO, promoted a return to Baal worship throughout 2019.

A replica of the Arch of Baal that stood at the entrance of the demonic temple in Palmyra, Syria, was transported and set up throughout Europe and also in Washington, D.C. The original Temple of Baal was built in the 3rd century before Christ. An arch that marked the entrance to this pagan shrine was constructed in 32 AD. The arch was all that remained of this pagan temple where so many children were sacrificed to the image of this foul idol. ISIS destroyed the original Arch in October 2015, but one year later, the Institute for Digital Archeology used 3D technology to reproduce a 20-foot full-scale replica. With great fanfare, the Arch of Baal was set up in Geneva, Switzerland, in front of the Palace of the Nations on April 12, 2019. This is where thousands of intergovernmental agencies from around the world meet and formulate the policies for global governance.

A replica of the Arch was unveiled on the National Mall in Washington, D.C. on October 1, 2018. At the unveiling ceremony, the chairman of the House Foreign Affairs Committee and the ranking member hailed the exhibition of the reconstructed Arch as the symbol of "global cultural heritage." Congressman Eliot Engle from New York said, "When you look at this beautiful Arch, we are seeing through the eyes of ancient civilizations, and to have it right here – set against the classical columns of the Capitol – is really extraordinary."[10] The congressman said more than he knew, because within a few short months, "extraordinary" events beset those countries that hosted this diabolical monument to Baal.

In April 2019, the altar of Baal was set up in Damascus, further increasing the world's admiration for this evil religion that brought the wrath of God on ancient civilizations. It is not a coincidence that just eight months after the Arch of Baal was set up in various capitals of the world, a lethal virus plagued the entire globe. All of the evidence for the origins of the virus point to a Chinese bio-weapons laboratory, but those with spiritual insight are aware that the Arch of Baal was really a point of entry for demonic powers who

---

10 Michael F. Haverluck, "The Arch of Baal erected in D.C. to Pagan's Delight," onenewsnow.com, 1 October 2018.

came with the assignment to make the virus a world-wide plague. Satan is behind every sickness, whether it is manufactured in a laboratory or a freak combination of natural phenomena. The bizarre reception given to this arch in national capitals actually put out the "welcome mat" for the return of Baal worship.

The coronavirus is not the only work of darkness that plagued the nation in 2019 and 2020. There were unprecedented riots from Antifa and BLM. Unprecedented corruption surfaced in the electoral process and judiciary. America's enemies gained new confidence to conduct cyber-warfare against us, and military tensions with Russia and Iran intensified. Socialists seized the government. Perversion seized the culture. Apathy seized the Church.

The Arch was originally an ancient doorway for principalities and devilish powers to enter the earth realm. Just months before the pandemic, a replica of that ancient obscenity was actually a portal for the wrecking crews of satan to pass into our country with their accelerated strategy to kill, steal, and destroy.

Now is the appointed time for believers with an Elijah anointing to come forward and proclaim, "Let the God that answers by fire, let Him be God!" The country is at a crossroads as ancient Israel was centuries ago. A fresh boldness from the Holy Ghost is coming on the Church to startle a confused populace and challenge the "woke" ideologies of a nation gone awry.

Multitudes have been on the proverbial fence long enough. Contrary to popular belief, there is no mixing between darkness and light, nor is there a happy medium between good and evil. There are no "grey areas" where people can retreat to hide their secret sin. All the efforts to fuse Biblical truth with godless philosophies have only increased the moral insanity which bring everlasting doom in a Christless eternity. It is decision time for the nation. "Let the God that answers by fire, let Him be God!"

The tense political and cultural conditions of our country rapidly degenerated once the Arch of Baal was erected on the National Mall in Washington D.C. The "defund police" movement sent crime to record levels. A riot at the nation's capital was used as an excuse to increase government control. The new administration enacted an historic number of executive orders designed to overturn America's Judeo-Christian values. It is telling that among the first executive orders issued by the occupant in the White House was an order to restore federal funding for abortion.

The spirit of Baal stepped through the Arch and has wreaked havoc on our country ever since. The Arch was actually a gateway for "principalities, powers, rulers of the darkness of this world, and spiritual wickedness in high places" to enter (Eph. 6:12). A door was opened to intense demonic activity and far worse monsters are yet to walk through it.

Whatever evil came through that Arch will be met with an anointing of the Holy Ghost that makes devilish agents bow at our feet. Our Savior's promise remains intact, "upon this rock I will build my church; and the gates of hell shall not prevail against it" (Matt. 16:18).

Elijah called down Heavenly fire and activated the sword that silenced the prophets of Baal in Israel. Today, believers with an "Elijah anointing" can do the same with the sword of the Spirit, the Word of God.

From a Scriptural standpoint, our nation is plagued with the same spiritual and moral maladies which brought ruin, captivity, and destruction to ancient Israel. The sinful belief system that hastened the demise of God's ancient people stemmed from the worship of Baal. Baal worship destroyed Israel's freedom, its prosperity, its blessings, and its peace. The practice of Baal worship made Israel vulnerable to its enemies and unleashed hellish conditions on the entire land. Baalism in the United States is called by such names as political correctness, liberalism, progressivism, universalism, Critical Race Theory, and wokeness. These ideologies advocate the same demonic practices and ideology of ancient Baal worship.

Baalism in ancient times was more than idolatry and a false religion; it was a mindset and a godless lifestyle.

Amorites, Moabites, Babylonians, Phoenicians, Canaanites and Egyptians worshipped this false god and fashioned their culture after its evil ways. Baal was the ancient progenitor of today's "nature" worship. He was called the "exalted lord of the earth—the rider of the clouds—the storm god—the god of war—the god of sex—the god of perversion." Jesus referred to satan as Baal-zebub—prince of demons. The territorial spirits that dominated cities and towns were called "the baals." The followers of Baal normalized homosexuality, incest, and every other abomination.

Baal worship was the author of pornography by depicting sex in hand-crafted large-as-life wooden objects and placing them in high places called "groves." Baal worshippers were the original abortionists, killing their newborns and infants in horrendous fires. Baal worship was really sexual entertainment replete with suggestive dancing and snake charming.

The followers of Baal made education a priority to indoctrinate their children in its evil belief system. Archeologists uncovered the ruins of extensive libraries and religious seminaries next to the temples of Baal. It was the followers of Baal in Phoenicia that invented the alphabet. The intellectuals of ancient times, just as the self-professed intellectuals of our time, gravitated to Baal worship as the means to material and political success.

The Israelites were repeatedly warned about the

evils of Baal worship. The Lord told them not to cavort, copy, mix, or imitate any of their practices or adopt their beliefs. The Hebrews were told that their only hope of surviving and thriving in the land was to utterly destroy the idolatrous system of Baal worship. Nothing of it was to be spared: the groves were to be cut down, their altars destroyed, their temples demolished, and their priests cut off. But instead of being obedient to the Word of the Lord, the Israelites repeatedly compromised and attempted to find some middle ground between the worship of the one true God and the practices of Baal. Baalism always led to Israel's downfall whenever they permitted themselves to be seduced by its perverted ways.

The Apostle Paul encapsulated all the wicked factors of ancient Baal worship in Romans chapter one. The factors which comprise Baalism were present in Roman idolatry in his time and now dominate the politically correct culture of our day. Romans 1:21-32:

> 21 Because that, when they knew God, they glorified him not as God, neither were thankful; but became vain in their imaginations, and their foolish heart was darkened.
>
> 22 Professing themselves to be wise, they became fools,
>
> 23 And changed the glory of the uncorruptible

God into an image made like to corruptible man, and to birds, and fourfooted beasts, and creeping things.

²⁴ Wherefore God also gave them up to uncleanness through the lusts of their own hearts, to dishonour their own bodies between themselves:

²⁵ Who changed the truth of God into a lie, and worshipped and served the creature more than the Creator, who is blessed for ever. Amen.

²⁶ For this cause God gave them up unto vile affections: for even their women did change the natural use into that which is against nature:

²⁷ And likewise also the men, leaving the natural use of the woman, burned in their lust one toward another; men with men working that which is unseemly, and receiving in themselves that recompence of their error which was meet.

²⁸ And even as they did not like to retain God in their knowledge, God gave them over to a reprobate mind, to do those things which are not convenient;

²⁹ Being filled with all unrighteousness, fornication, wickedness, covetousness, maliciousness;

full of envy, murder, debate, deceit, malignity; whisperers,

30 Backbiters, haters of God, despiteful, proud, boasters, inventors of evil things, disobedient to parents,

31 Without understanding, covenantbreakers, without natural affection, implacable, unmerciful:

32 Who knowing the judgment of God, that they which commit such things are worthy of death, not only do the same, but have pleasure in them that do them.

Baal worshippers invented a number of superstitions about the sun and moon. They believed the heavenly bodies were actually deities that intended to harm human beings. They believed that the sun's summer heat was an attempt to attack people in the daytime, and the moon would smite with madness in the night. The Holy Spirit wanted His covenant people to know that none of the lies of Baal could harm them. So He inspired the Psalmist to write in Psalm 121:6-8:

6 The sun shall not smite thee by day, nor the moon by night.

7 The Lord shall preserve thee from all evil: he shall preserve thy soul.

[8] The LORD shall preserve thy going out and thy coming in from this time forth, and even for evermore.

By their obedience to the Word of God, the Lord's covenant people got victory over Baal and discovered that "no weapon formed against them could prosper" (Isa. 54:17).

The Lord was specific about the judgments that were sent against the followers of Baal. Zephaniah outlined the peculiar phenomenon that comes on the land which defiles itself with the practices of Baal. A distinctive set of judgments is unleashed which starts with the mysterious death of wildlife for no apparent reason. Zephaniah 1:3-4, "...I will consume the fowls of the heaven, and the fishes of the sea, and the stumbling blocks with the wicked: and I will cut off man from off the land, saith the Lord...I will cut off the remnant of Baal from this place..."

In recent years, hundreds of birds have fallen dead from the sky in various states, and fish died by the thousands in lakes, rivers, and the coastlines. It is not uncommon to periodically hear of the mysterious death of wildlife in various parts of the country. Not long ago, there were reports of hundreds of dead fish washing up on the shores of Galveston Beach, Texas. Just days prior to this strange event, thousands of fish died in the rivers of Nebraska, Illinois, and Iowa. There were so many dead fish in one Illinois lake that the carcasses clogged an intake screen near a power plant.

The Holy Spirit recorded in Zephaniah 1:6-7 that this freak happening in nature is a precursor to the calamities that will come on "them that are turned back from the LORD; and those that have not sought the LORD, nor enquired for him."

The prophet Jeremiah revealed that stealing, murder, adultery, lying, and corruption descend on a nation dominated by the practices of Baal. The Jews believed that they could serve Baal during the week and then worship God on the Sabbath, but discovered that their self-deception was lethal. It is written in Jeremiah 7:9-10, 15:

> [9] Will ye steal, murder, and commit adultery, and swear falsely, and burn incense unto Baal, and walk after other gods whom ye know not;
>
> [10] And come and stand before me in this house, which is called by my name, and say, We are delivered (permitted) to do all these abominations?
>
> [15] I will cast you out of my sight...

To avoid unprecedented calamities and catastrophes, we must have a BAAL OUT! The influences of Baal must be destroyed. It will take a Church rising up with "the spirit and power of Elijah" to fight the good fight of faith and defeat the nefarious forces mobilized against us.

The chief promoter of the world tour of the Arch of Baal stated, "The Palmyra Arch is an open gate, offering the opportunity to pass through and look to the future."[11] The future Mr. Berkowitz envisions is a world dominated by the same mindset of ancient Baal worshippers. It is a totalitarian nightmare where genocide and human sacrifice (abortion, euthanasia, etc.) are accepted as the new norm. It is a culture defined by detestable abominations.

The stark choice that looms before our nation and our churches is either we turn back to the Bible or back to Baal. Communities, families, and the Body of Christ are waiting for someone to tear down Baal's altar in the "spirit and power of Elijah." We don't have much time. "...Now is the accepted time; behold, now is the day of salvation" (II Cor. 6:2). The response of every believer in this present crisis is to pick up the mantle, rebuild the altar, call fire down from Heaven, and intercede in prayer until the cloud appears to end the long spiritual drought. The sound of an abundance of rain is getting louder, but only those with the "spirit and power of Elijah" will hear and experience it.

---

11 Adam Eliyahu Berkowitz, eyeopeningtruth.com, 27 April 2019.

CONCLUSION

The "spirit and power" of Elijah is a special anointing of the Holy Ghost that appears on God's messengers just before a time of unprecedented upheaval. This divine endowment of power is especially connected with the appearance of Messiah. John the Baptist was the forerunner of Jesus who announced the first coming of the Lord. Jesus identified John as that generation's Elijah. He said, "...Elias (Elijah) truly shall first come, and restore all things. But I say unto you, That Elias is come already, and they knew him not..." (Matt. 17:11-12).

The angel Gabriel made it clear to the father of John the Baptist that his son would not be Elijah, but minister before the Lord "in the spirit and power of Elias...to make ready a people prepared for the Lord" (Luke 1:17).

Elijah will be sent back to Israel during Tribulation times to announce the second coming of Jesus. His message will be punctuated with miracles of deliverance and judgment. He and the other witness will supernaturally hinder the plans of antichrist until the world ruler succeeds in executing God's two prophets in the streets of

Jerusalem. Television cameras from every network will beam images of their d̶e̶a̶d̶ ̶b̶o̶dies by satellite to every nation on ea̶r̶t̶h̶.̶ ̶c̶e̶l̶l̶ phones will see these events in real time. The "woke" global culture will celebrate the murder of God's two messengers and tout their deaths as proof that man has finally defeated God.

But the merrymaking will be short lived, because three and half days into the celebration, "the spirit of life from God entered into them, and they stood on their feet; and great fear fell upon them which saw them" (Rev. 11:11). Elijah will complete the ministry which God suspended centuries ago, and then he will ascend into Heaven in a cloud as enemies look on (Rev. 11:12).

Malachi's prophecy concludes the Old Testament with the promise, "Behold, I will send you Elijah the prophet before the coming of the great and dreadful day of the Lord" (Mal. 4:5). John the Baptist ministered a short time before the crucifixion and resurrection of Jesus. He did more than identify the Messiah, he exposed the evil policies of a government that would soon destroy his nation. A great and dreadful day of unprecedented destruction was coming. In 70 AD, the Romans committed genocide against the Jews and scattered the survivors to the ends of the earth.

There is no worse "great and dreadful day" than the coming seven years of Tribulation. The upheaval in nature, the advent of mysterious diseases, the deployment of nuclear weapons, the food shortages, the loss of freedom, the bizarre weather, the massive deceptions, the genocide, the evils of a world government, and the grotesque abominations of an irredeemable society will be beyond belief.

The prophetic Word of God details all of these factors as dominating the culture even before Tribulation begins. The Lord instructed us that when these things begin to come to pass, we are to look up, because "our redemption draweth nigh" (Luke 21:28). Jesus is soon to appear in the clouds. Since the Coming of the Lord is so close, the Holy Ghost will resort to extreme measures in a final effort to awaken people to the nearness of the Lord's Return. He will commission sons and daughters to prophesy and foretell the calamity that is coming.

The unique empowerment of the Holy Ghost upon "sons and daughters" in these last days will be equal to the anointing on Elijah when he opposed King Ahab and contested against the prophets of Baal. The measure of heavenly power released on God's Church in these Endtimes will carry the same boldness that was on John when he indicted King Herod for the evil of his administration.

Today, believers are faced with the evil of Marxist globalism which is far more sinister and deadly than any past Nazi, Communist, or Fascist regime. The person whom the Bible calls "antichrist" is waiting in the wings and looking for the right moment to step forward with his deceptive plan for world peace. But the power that motivates the antichrist is not political, economic, social, or cultural. The "man of sin" functions by demonic power which can only be overcome and hindered as the Holy Ghost works through anointed believers.

All Bible believers should note that the first and second comings of Messiah are both preceded by the "spirit and power of Elijah." Since the Lord is soon to appear in the clouds, we can expect "the spirit and power of Elijah" to be manifested once more, enabling us to successfully fight against the influences of modern Baal worship.

The "spirit and power of Elijah" is more than a man, it is a movement. The Word of God defines Elijah's ministry as a ministry of restoration. Jesus said that Elijah "restoreth all things" (Mark 9:12). The "spirit and power of Elijah" will bring the time foretold by the Apostle Peter in Acts 3:21, "Whom the heaven must receive [Jesus] until the times of restitution [restoration] of all things, which God hath spoken by the mouth of all his holy prophets since the world [age] began."

The restoration of New Testament worship, power, breakthrough, joy, holiness, and glory is the purpose of the Elijah anointing before the "great and dreadful day of the Lord."

As all the Endtime signs emerge, and the spirit of

antichrist darkens our time, believers should not forget the Elijah factor. Just as Elijah centuries ago suddenly burst on the scene to announce the status quo would forever change, God has made available to believers special anointings which will redeem the time.

"Let the God that answers by fire, let Him be God."

CPSIA information can be obtained
at www.ICGtesting.com
Printed in the USA
LVHW031726231021
701301LV00001B/2